The ECB and the Euro:
the First Five Years

The ECB and the Euro: the First Five Years

PROFESSOR OTMAR ISSING

WITH A COMMENTARY BY DAVID B. SMITH

The Institute of Economic Affairs

First published in Great Britain in 2004 by
The Institute of Economic Affairs
2 Lord North Street
Westminster
London SW1P 3LB
in association with Profile Books Ltd

The mission of the Institute of Economic Affairs is to improve public understanding of the fundamental institutions of a free society, with particular reference to the role of markets in solving economic and social problems.

A CIP catalogue record for this book is available from the British Library.

ISBN 0 255 36555 1

Many IEA publications are translated into languages other than English or are reprinted. Permission to translate or to reprint should be sought from the Director General at the address above.

Typeset in Stone by MacGuru Ltd
info@macguru.org.uk

Printed and bound in Great Britain by Hobbs the Printers

CONTENTS

THE AUTHOR

Professor Otmar Issing, who was born in 1936, has been a member of the Executive Board of the European Central Bank since 1 June 1998. The business area for which he is responsible includes the Directorates of General Economics and Research. Until May 1998 he was a member of the board of the Deutsche Bundesbank with a seat on the Central Bank Council. Prior to that he held chairs of economics at the Universities of Würzburg and Erlangen-Nürnberg. In 1991 he was awarded an honorary professorship at the University of Würzburg. From 1988 to 1990 he was a member of the Council of Experts for the Assessment of Overall Economic Developments. He is an active member of the Akademie der Wissenschaften und der Literatur (Academy of Sciences and Literature), Mainz, and of the Academia Scientiarum et Artium Europaea (European Academy of Sciences and Arts). In addition to publishing numerous articles in scientific journals and periodicals, he is the author of, *inter alia*, two textbooks, namely *Einführung in die Geldtheorie* (Introduction to Monetary Theory), thirteenth edition, 2003, and *Einführung in die Geldpolitik* (Introduction to Monetary Policy), sixth edition, 1996.

FOREWORD

Previous IEA authors have often expressed scepticism about the case for the UK joining the euro zone. One objection that has been levelled is that the adoption of the euro in Britain would reduce currency competition: indeed, it would be a decisive move towards a money monopoly in the European Union. Nevertheless, it might still be the case that adopting the euro is beneficial for the majority of countries in the EU, even if it is not good for the UK. Furthermore, if one accepts the currency competition argument, a well-managed euro might still be good for those countries that choose to maintain their own currencies, such as the UK, just as the maintenance of alternative currencies benefits the euro area.

The currency competition argument has at least two strands. The first is that the ability of citizens of one country to use a currency that is not their own imposes a discipline on the government of that country to create effective monetary institutions. *In extremis*, people would start to use an alternative currency if their own currency was badly managed. The second strand is that monetary authorities can learn from each other's practices and mistakes.

Professor Otmar Issing, member of the Executive Board of the European Central Bank (ECB), makes a strong case that the euro has been well managed since its introduction. The ECB understands and learns from the practices of other central banks. But the success of the ECB in achieving its objective of price stability suggests that this learning process can work in the other direction too. In Occasional Paper 134, Issing discusses the considerable uncertainty that existed at the beginning of the euro project. There were not only technical challenges of a nature and scale not previously encountered but also the major economic challenge of conducting a monetary policy appropriate for the whole euro area.

It was essential for the ECB to establish credibility quickly once it began to implement the single monetary policy. Markets needed to be assured that the goal of price stability would be achieved. Issing shows that there was a genuine intellectual commitment to that goal and that, despite not following an explicit inflation or monetary target, it was possible for the ECB to establish credibility using its two-pillar economic strategy. Issing explains why he believes that inflation targeting is not appropriate for the euro area – and indeed his arguments apply to any monetary area – and discusses the important role of monetary policy in the ECB's thinking. Indeed, monetary variables and monetary instruments probably play a more prominent role in the ECB's strategy than they do in the Bank of England's strategy for maintaining inflation around its target level.

Issing goes on to show how the ECB coped well with different types of economic shocks in 1999 and 2001. He comments, 'Whenever it has been confronted with new economic conditions, the Governing Council of the ECB has not hesitated to take resolute action to pursue a policy that best serves the purpose of maintaining price stability in the medium term.' He then goes on to suggest that long-term inflation expectations have been anchored at a level consistent with price stability. Issing suggests that this, together with increased understanding of the mandate and policy of the ECB, is an important measure of the ECB's success.

The ECB and the Euro: the First Five Years concludes on a cautionary note. There are structural rigidities in the euro zone, notes Issing, particularly in the labour market. These are the cause of slow growth and high unemployment. It is essential that governments are mindful of their responsibilities to reform these areas of policy and that the ECB is not asked to do what it cannot do – that is, rectify the poor growth and employment records caused by these rigidities.

Issing's paper is followed by a commentary by David B. Smith, Chief Economist at Williams de Broë and chairman of the IEA's Shadow Monetary Policy Committee. Smith is highly complimentary about the ECB's achievements. He suggests that the success of the ECB in using monetary growth as a key leading indicator of inflation could have lessons for the UK. At the end of his commentary Smith asks whether the success of the ECB should persuade the UK to join the euro zone. He suggests that it should not, because the political implications of joining the euro would lead, in the long term, to serious economic consequences.

The ECB and the Euro: the First Five Years was first presented as the 2004 Mais Lecture at Sir John Cass Business School. The IEA is pleased to publish the lecture as part of its programme. The relationship between the IEA and Sir John Cass Business School has always been informal but very fruitful, and this lecture and the commentary commissioned by the IEA form an important contribution to the debate on monetary policy.

The views expressed in Occasional Paper 134 are, as in all IEA publications, those of the author and not those of the Institute

(which has no corporate view), its managing trustees, Academic
Advisory Council members or senior staff.

PHILIP BOOTH

Editorial and Programme Director,
Institute of Economic Affairs
Professor of Insurance and Risk Management,
Sir John Cass Business School, City University
November 2004

ACKNOWLEDGEMENTS

The author is grateful to Dr Claus Brand for his invaluable assistance. The IEA is grateful to Sir John Cass Business School, and in particular to Professor Geoffrey Wood, for the opportunity to publish Sir John Cass Business School's 2004 Mais Lecture.

SUMMARY

- The adoption of the euro by twelve EU countries presented a unique challenge for monetary policy, but today the euro is established as a stable currency, appreciated by investors worldwide.
- The adoption of the euro was made significantly easier by the substantial convergence of the EU economies in the late 1990s.
- In order to establish credibility, a systematic framework was necessary to assess the economic situation and future risks to price stability in the euro zone. Independence from political institutions is also important for credibility.
- The ECB is charged with maintaining price stability and it has been the Governing Council of the ECB which has translated this objective into the practical policy of maintaining inflation in the medium term below, but close to, 2 per cent.
- The ECB has not been given an explicit inflation target by its political masters as the Bank of England has been. Also, the ECB does not pursue monetary targeting.
- The ECB has a two-pillar approach to its analytical work, conducting both a monetary analysis and a more general economic analysis. Arguably, monetary analysis plays a more explicit role than it does in the Bank of England's economic analysis.

- Accountability and transparency are essential if the ECB is to maintain credibility. The success of the ECB in maintaining credibility is indicated by the extent to which long-term interest rates are consistent with the ECB's interpretation of price stability – that is, consistent with future inflation of 2 per cent. More generally, the ECB enjoys a very high degree of credibility in the markets: there is confidence that the ECB can deliver its objectives.
- The ECB has been faced with a number of economic shocks and has dealt with these effectively.
- There is concern about slow growth and low employment in the euro area. These problems arise as a result of structural rigidities, especially in the labour market. It is essential that these issues are addressed by member governments and EU institutions. It is important that EU governments do not expect the ECB to solve these problems as it is not within its power to do so.

TABLES AND FIGURES

TABLES AND FIGURES

The ECB and the Euro:
the First Five Years

1 A NEW CENTRAL BANK AND A NEW CURRENCY

The European Central Bank (ECB) was established on 1 June 1998. Seven months later, on 1 January 1999, eleven European countries transferred monetary sovereignty to the new institution and the ECB started conducting a single monetary policy for what has become the euro area.

The European Monetary Union was a unique project. Although the process of preparing for the adoption of the single currency had led to a degree of convergence that many had not thought possible, the sceptics were anything but convinced. One central bank, a single monetary policy and eleven sovereign national governments with policies centred on national interests – how could this be expected to work? How was it going to be possible to successfully formulate a monetary policy for a new and still diverse currency area and establish the euro as a stable currency? Observers considered a whole range of different scenarios, from the euro as a panacea for all of Europe's economic ills to the collapse of the single currency.

The adoption of a common currency by twelve European countries presented a unique challenge for monetary policy. In 1998 the ECB announced a monetary policy strategy explaining how it aimed to pursue price stability. This strategy has proved to be superior to the alternatives. Consequently, in the evaluation of its strategy in May 2003, the Governing Council of the ECB confirmed that it aimed to maintain inflation below, but close to, 2 per cent over the medium term and that its decisions would continue to be based on a comprehensive economic and monetary analysis of risks to price stability.

Today the euro has not merely survived: it is firmly established as a stable currency and is appreciated by investors worldwide. Against the background of all the concerns expressed, and in the light of the experience gained over those first five years, it is time to take stock.

This monograph provides a discussion of key aspects of the launch of the single European currency and the conduct of monetary policy in the euro area. In Chapter 2 it reviews economic questions that were of primary concern prior to and, ultimately, at the very time of the introduction of the euro. These relate to whether the euro area can be considered an optimum currency area and the extent to which the fulfilment of the convergence criteria was conducive to enhancing the credibility of the monetary integration process. Chapter 3 looks at the key elements of the ECB's monetary policy strategy. It reassesses the considerations underlying the definition of price stability and discusses the framework for internal analysis and decision-making that encompasses the ECB's economic and monetary analysis. Especially with regard to the role of money and the ECB's medium-term orientation, it considers to what extent this approach differs from inflation targeting strategies. Chapter 4 provides an overview of the operational procedures used by the ECB to implement monetary policy decisions. In view of the need for transparency and accountability arising from the political independence granted to the ECB, Chapter 5 discusses key aspects of the ECB's communication with the public. Chapter 6 concludes by assessing to what extent the ECB has been successful in discharging its primary obligation of maintaining price stability and anchoring inflation expectations.

2 A NEW CURRENCY – A NEW CENTRAL BANK – A NEW CURRENCY AREA

Uncertainty surrounding the new currency area

When the ECB initially came to implement the single monetary policy, it faced a whole string of specific uncertainties (Issing et al., 2001; Issing, 2002a and 2002b). One such uncertainty, which all central banks typically face, concerned the way in which the transmission mechanism – that is, the process by which changes in monetary conditions affect the price level – would function. This problem was especially relevant for the ECB when monetary union was in its infancy. The transmission of monetary policy impulses to prices and economic activity is, of course, subject to considerable time lags, the precise duration of which can only be estimated. Knowledge of the way in which an economy functions is typically limited to a rough approximation of certain aspects of the transmission mechanism on the basis of various models. Moreover, the parameters of these models can never be determined with complete certainty. Initially, the transmission mechanism for the future currency area could at best be assessed only in vague terms. It was also anticipated that the transmission mechanism might alter decisively with the introduction of the euro and the single monetary policy on 1 January 1999. The transition to a single European currency constitutes a classic example of the famous 'Lucas

Critique' (Lucas, 1976), which states that a change in policy can influence economic actors' behavioural patterns, thereby altering the parameters of the models that have until that point been used to, among other things, determine the transmission mechanism. For example, the transition to the single currency had the potential to change the structure of financial markets and the extent of competition among banks. The consequences of the regime shift as regards the structure of the financial sector and competition in the banking system could then affect the transmission of monetary policy impulses through the economy.[1]

Another source of uncertainty which central banks typically have to face was particularly acute in relation to the introduction of the new single currency: the assessment of the economic situation on the basis of macroeconomic data. Particularly at the outset, the Governing Council had only a very limited set of reliable harmonised macroeconomic data at its disposal. Some important data were not available at all for the euro area,[2] while other data were available only with considerable time lags and, in addition, were potentially subject to extensive revision. Now, however, more timely and reliable harmonised macroeconomic time series are available, and these series extend back farther into

[1] For current evidence of possible changes to the transmission mechanism on account of the introduction of the single currency, see Angeloni and Ehrmann (2003).

[2] This was true in particular for historical series covering the entire euro area. Econometric analysis – for example of the transmission mechanism – has to be carried out on the basis of synthetic historical data for the period prior to the establishment of monetary union. The data are aggregated on the basis of national data. The chosen methods of aggregation remain controversial. In this regard, see Fagan, Henry and Mestre (2001); Beyer, Doornik and Hendry (2001); and Brand, Gerdesmeier and Roffia (2002: 27–9, 56–8).

the past. Nevertheless, by comparison with the USA, for example, the position of the ECB as regards data still cannot be considered completely satisfactory.

In these circumstances it was necessary to develop a strategy that would be distinguished primarily by a high degree of robustness in the face of such an exceptional confluence of risks.

Does one size fit all?

The start of monetary union on 1 January 1999 brought together quite unique challenges for economic and monetary policy. For decades, the process of European integration had been the subject of intense discussion in the economic literature, in which the general consensus was that the euro area, comprising the eleven – and now twelve – participating member states, was *ex ante* not an optimum currency area (Bayoumi and Eichengreen, 1993a and 1993b). Critical observers therefore took the view that the single monetary policy was doomed to failure. In addition, the existence of autonomous national fiscal policies was considered incompatible with a supranational monetary policy. Finally, there was considerable concern at the institutional level that the decentralised organisation of the Eurosystem would cause national interests to dominate the implementation of monetary policy and ultimately lead to constant conflict between the Executive Board and the Governing Council. Many observers claimed that the six members of the Executive Board, representing the 'euro area view', would be overruled by the initially eleven (now twelve) governors of the national central banks, who would seek to promote the interests of their respective countries. None of these fears has materialised. Since then, and not least since the introduction of the euro banknotes and coins, the euro has become part of people's daily lives. This is not to say, however, that scepticism has disappeared completely.

The success of the single monetary policy is crucially dependent on the probability of significant asymmetric shocks and on the extent to which the regions affected are considered flexible in the sense that product and factor markets are able to respond effectively to price signals. Linguistic and cultural factors mean that labour mobility in the euro area is relatively limited by comparison with other large currency areas, and this can make it difficult to adapt to asymmetric shocks (Blanchard and Katz, 1992). In these circumstances, it is even more important that there be sufficient flexibility in the goods and factor markets. In particular in the labour market, the euro area is still – even after nearly five years of monetary union – far from being an optimum currency area.

The question of whether one size fits all also relates to the question of whether a single monetary policy will, on account of the diverse nature of the currency area, give rise to permanently asynchronous economic cycles (see Bayoumi and Eichengreen, 1993a and 1993b). It appears questionable, however, whether the factors that were important in that respect in the preparations for monetary union will continue to apply in the future. Historically observed inflation differentials, and differences between economic cycles on account of asymmetric shocks, have many sources, and monetary integration can be expected to diminish the effect of these.[3] One of the principal causes of asymmetric shocks – namely

---

3   According to Rogers (2001), for example, only 0.33 per cent of the difference between the Irish rate of inflation and the European average in 1999 was attributable to price convergence, with the remainder being attributable to demand factors. Alesina et al. (2001) likewise attach greater importance to demand factors.

the effects of divergent national monetary policies – no longer exists (Bayoumi and Eichengreen, 1993a). Furthermore, it is to be expected that the creation of a single market and a single currency will lead to deeper trade integration and help to increase price transparency, thereby reducing the extent to which different prices can be charged in different countries for the same goods or services.[4] Increased competition in the goods and factor markets will lead to the further alignment of economic cycles.

It should be noted that research on monetary policy transmission in the euro area has made great progress,[5] with important contributions from both academics and experts within the Eurosystem. Their findings provide no clear evidence of any significant differences in the way that monetary policy affects the various participating member states. In any event, the differences that were identified were not robust to changes in the method, models or time series used. The above-mentioned factors contributing to economic divergence in the euro area can certainly not be regarded as a given, and it is to be expected that the deepening of financial market integration will also entail a convergence in the transmission of monetary policy impulses (Atkeson and Bayoumi, 1993).

Structural differences, which make it difficult for national or regional rates of inflation to converge over the longer term, are likewise not necessarily static. Neither do they automatically pose a problem where monetary policy is concerned. Inflation differentials are usually associated with the Balassa-Samuelson effect (see

---

4   See also Rogers (2001), according to which price differentials in the euro area are roughly the same as in the United States. See also ECB (2003a and 2003d).

5   For an overview of the Eurosystem's analysis of the transmission mechanism, see Angeloni, Kashyap and Mojon (2003).

Balassa, 1964; Samuelson, 1964), according to which long-term differentials in regional inflation are attributable to differences in the rate at which productivity increases in the various regions' tradable and non-tradable goods sectors. A currency area may experience such inflation differentials if it includes countries with a lower standard of living that are in the process of catching up with the others. As living standards converge, however, the effect of these differentials declines.[6]

The combination of these factors means that a set of criteria relating to the theory of what constitutes an optimum currency area that were not met *ex ante* may well be fulfilled in the process of, and, indeed, partly as a result of the process of, monetary union, so that they do become fulfilled *ex post*. In that respect they are endogenous – rather than exogenous – determinants (Issing, 2001).

Real and nominal convergence

At the same time it must not be overlooked that all countries that joined the euro had made considerable progress in monetary policy by the time of entry. Fulfilment of the convergence criteria was a prerequisite for participation.

In 1991, at the EU Council meeting in Maastricht, the heads of state or government agreed on a set of nominal and practically applicable criteria that would be applied to select those countries that would become members of the single currency area. These economic convergence criteria, relating to price stability,

---

6   For an overview, see Camba-Méndez (2003). For an overview of the causes of inflation differentials in the euro area, see ECB (2003d).

Figure 1 **HICP inflation in participating countries prior to Stage Three of EMU (annual percentage changes)**

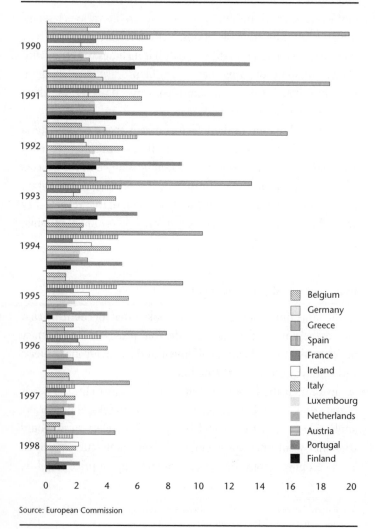

Source: European Commission

Figure 2   **Government surpluses/deficits of participating countries prior to Stage Three of EMU (% of GDP)**

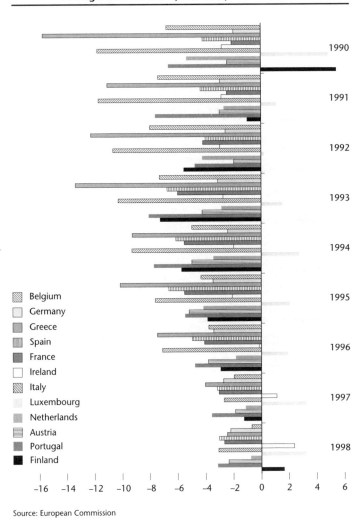

Source: European Commission

Figure 3 **Government debt of participating countries prior to Stage Three of EMU (% of GDP)**

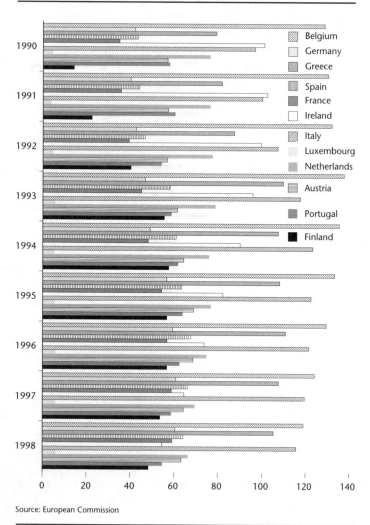

Source: European Commission

public finances, exchange rate stability and long-term interest rates, whilst also taking into account a number of other factors, such as the degree of market integration, were designed in such a way as to act as indicators of the extent to which the prospective member countries would be able to sustain stability-oriented economic policies. A further criterion stipulates that member states' legislation should be consistent with the provisions on central bank independence contained in the treaties establishing the European Community. The philosophy that dictated the selection of the macroeconomic criteria was that countries able to sustain stability-oriented policies marked by low inflation and sound public finances are less likely to experience substantial internal economic problems, which in a single currency area could have negative spillover effects to other countries. Exchange rate stability and low long-term interest rates have been serving as a market test of the success in achieving stability-oriented policies.

The convergence criteria were thus formulated with great clarity. They were key to ensuring the credibility of the monetary integration process and successfully served as a target and disciplining device for economic policies in EU member states throughout the 1990s. In fact, right from the start of EMU they resulted in a historically high degree of monetary and fiscal stability, whilst also preparing countries for the realities of life in a single currency area. Figures 1 to 3 show how inflation, government borrowing and government debt all decreased, in some cases significantly, in the period before monetary union. With the benefit of hindsight, it is difficult to imagine that the process of disinflation and fiscal consolidation in Europe in the 1990s would have been possible without the clarity of the convergence criteria or the prospect of monetary union. As many as eleven countries were able to fulfil the criteria ahead of the start of Stage Three of EMU in 1999 – a scenario that had not been expected only a few years before – while Greece was also able to join the euro area in 2001.

3 MANDATE AND STRATEGY OF THE ECB

Main elements of the strategy

All the factors of uncertainty identified above confronted monetary policy with completely new challenges. In a situation of such extreme uncertainty it was necessary, first and foremost, to do everything possible to avoid major mistakes. At the same time a clear and convincing commitment by the ECB to its primary objective was vital. In those circumstances, and not least because of the ECB's lack of a track record, it was simply inconceivable for the single monetary policy to be pursued on a purely discretionary, ad hoc basis. A systematic framework was therefore needed in order to assess the economic situation and future risks to price stability, one that could also be used for decision-making and communication. The announcement of such an approach, i.e. a monetary policy strategy, had to be consistent with the public commitment to maintain price stability.

In 1997, before I had the slightest idea about my later appointment and responsibility, I outlined the specific challenge for the future ECB as follows:

> [e]xperience has shown that central banks are most likely to
> be credible if they have a successful, stability-oriented track
> record. [...] Unfortunately, the European Central Bank
> does not have the option of referring to a successful past

[...]. It is extremely important, in order to stabilise inflation expectations, that the ECB proves from the start that it is capable of achieving its primary objective. The sooner it can gain credibility and trust in that way, the easier its task will become and the more difficult it would be for inflation expectations to develop and take hold. That stabilisation will also depend to a large extent on the ECB having a convincing and transparent strategy which makes clear its policy of ensuring stability and which the ECB itself can use as a guide. (Issing, 1998: 184–90)

In October 1998 – that is to say well before the responsibility for monetary policy passed from the national central banks to the ECB – the Governing Council decided on a stability-oriented strategy that would meet these requirements (ECB, 1998). The strategy was based on fundamental theoretical considerations and empirical knowledge, as well as on decades of policy experience acquired by the national central banks (see Issing et al., 2001). When the ECB's strategy was evaluated in 2003, it was necessary to review these considerations in the light of the experience gained over the first four and a half years of monetary policy. This assessment resulted in a reaffirmation by the Governing Council of the main elements of the strategy.

As indicated above, the treaty establishing the European Community makes price stability the primary objective of the ECB (Article 105(1)). The treaty gives no indication, however, of how exactly this is to be understood. In October 1998 the ECB chose to specify its mandate by announcing a quantitative definition of price stability. It thereby sought to establish a solid anchor for inflation expectations and set a benchmark which the public could use to hold the ECB accountable. Price stability was defined as a year-on-year increase in the Harmonised Index of Consumer Prices (HICP) for the euro area of below 2 per cent. The ECB also made it clear that price stability was to be maintained in the medium term (see ECB, 1998). The ECB's pursuit of price stability in the medium term recognises that monetary policy cannot control price developments in the short term and should not therefore seek to do so.

A number of observers regarded that definition as excessively ambitious and, furthermore, as asymmetrical,[1] since it did not lay down a specific lower bound for the rate of price increases. The use of the term 'increase', however, made it clear from the outset that, as with inflation, extended periods of deflation are not compatible with price stability either. The upper bound for price increases was – at 2 per cent – set some way above zero, providing a safety margin to guard against deflation. The ECB, not least as a result of uncertainty concerning the possible extent of any measurement bias in the HICP and in view of the possibility of temporal fluctuations in that index, did not define a specific lower bound for the rate of price increases.

The principal considerations that led to this definition were the subject of further critical assessment when the Governing Council evaluated the strategy, the outcome of which was published on 8 May 2003. The Governing Council, in line with the prior implementation of its policy, reaffirmed – as indicated above – the explicit quantitative definition of price stability. It also made clear that, over the medium term, its monetary policy would seek to achieve an inflation rate of 'below, but close to, 2 per cent' (ECB, 2003a and 2003b). The Governing Council thereby highlighted

---

1   See European Economic Advisory Group (2003); Fitoussi and Creel (2002); De Grauwe (2002); Svensson (2002 and 2003); IMF (2002); and Sachverständigenrat (2002).

its determination to maintain a sufficient safety margin to guard against deflationary risks. This margin is at the same time sufficient to take account of any measurement bias in the HICP and the effects of inflation differentials within the euro area. Aiming at inflation rates below, but close to, the upper bound as laid down by this definition is completely in line with the monetary policy pursued by the ECB in the past. It is also consistent with the markets' understanding of this policy. This is reflected in the long-term inflation expectations in the euro area, which from the outset have fluctuated between approximately 1.7 and 1.9 per cent (see also Figure 6).

Considerations regarding the definition of price stability

The choice of price index

A number of features were relevant to the choice of price index. The index was to be comprehensible to the public (transparency) and not subject to excessively frequent revision (reliability). Furthermore, it was to be available with sufficient timeliness and frequency, if possible on a monthly basis. The ECB, seeking a price index that met these criteria, chose in 1998 to define price stability in terms of the Harmonised Index of Consumer Prices (HICP), as calculated by Eurostat. Many observers called for price stability to be defined in terms of a core inflation rate that filtered out the more volatile components from the index.[2] This was rejected (see the July 2001 issue of the ECB's *Monthly Bulletin* for further discussion of this). It was rejected first on the grounds of transparency:

---

2   See, *inter alia*, Gros et al. (2001) and Alesina et al. (2001).

the fact that there were differing views on what constituted 'core inflation' would have made the choice of a specific core inflation measure look arbitrary. Furthermore, most of these concepts cannot be easily understood by the public. Second, the ECB is responsible for maintaining the purchasing power of the single currency as a whole, not just for partial indicators of purchasing power. The need to keep fundamental price trends in line with price stability was reflected in the decision to adopt a medium-term monetary policy stance.

The costs of inflation

When establishing a quantitative definition of price stability it was necessary to balance the costs of inflation against possible reasons for tolerating low positive rates of inflation. The welfare-reducing effects of inflation, identified in numerous studies, are well known, even if these effects are difficult to measure: the disruption of the allocation of resources through the distortion of relative prices; the effect of the level of inflation on uncertainty surrounding inflation and associated risk premiums in long-term interest rates; the exacerbation of the distortionary effects of taxation; the artificial expansion of the financial sector and other wasting of resources. These occur *inter alia* because economic actors reduce their money holdings in order to protect themselves against real wealth losses caused by inflation. Costs are also incurred as a result of the price changes themselves (menu costs). Finally, inflation has an effect on the distribution of income and wealth, not least between creditors and debtors. (On the costs of inflation, see Feldstein, 1997 and 1999; Fischer, 1981; ECB, 2001; and the overview in Rodríguez-Palenzuela, Camba-Méndez and García, 2003.)

Empirical analysis confirms that even low rates of inflation give rise to considerable costs in terms of welfare losses. The various causes of such welfare losses can be analysed in full using dynamic general equilibrium models, now common in monetary theory. The results of these studies suggest that the costs of inflation may be higher than previously thought and that even moderate rates of inflation imply considerable costs (for an overview, see Rodríguez-Palenzuela, Camba-Méndez and García, 2003). In a model calibrated for US data, Dotsey and Ireland (1996) show, for example, that if the rate of inflation rises from 0 to 4 per cent and then remains at that level, this will give rise to long-term welfare losses in the order of 0.4 to 1.1 per cent of output. These figures are considerably higher than those of older studies based on assessments providing only a partial analysis (such as Fischer, 1981; Lucas, 1981). One would normally conclude, on the basis of these general equilibrium models, that price stability in the true sense of the term (i.e. zero inflation) would be desirable from a welfare perspective.

Reasons for tolerating positive rates of inflation

There are, however, several factors that militate in favour of basing the definition of price stability – the objective of monetary policy – on a positive, but low, rate of inflation. One fundamental reason for doing so lies in the fact that nominal interest rates cannot normally sink beneath zero – the zero bound. The nearer the target inflation rate is to zero, the greater the risk that central banks might be unable to react sufficiently to deflationary shocks by reducing interest rates. Thus the zero bound is associated with considerable economic risks: sustained deflation can further exacerbate any existing financial instability, not least by increasing the real debt burden of private households and firms.

If the shock were severe enough, the economy could even be pushed into a deflationary spiral, in which price falls accelerate because the nominal interest rates have reached the zero lower bound, and the real interest rate therefore increases as deflation reaches higher rates (see Coenen, 2003a and 2003b; Klaeffling and Lopez, 2003; and the overview in Yates, 2002). If, on the other hand, the central bank's target in the medium term is not zero inflation, but rather a low, positive rate of price increases, the nominal interest rate will, with a given real equilibrium interest rate, also rise. This provides greater scope for reacting to negative demand shocks by means of interest rate reductions. Numerous studies indicate that the probability of reaching the zero lower bound is greatly reduced where central banks aim to maintain the inflation rate above 1 per cent (see Coenen, 2003b; Klaeffling and Lopez, 2003; and Orphanides and Wieland, 1998).[3]

A further factor in favour of tolerating low, positive levels of inflation is the possible existence of a positive measurement bias in the calculation of the consumer price index, which can arise in particular as a result of inadequate compensation for improvements in the quality of goods in the underlying basket. Although

---

[3]   This also reflects the practices of the central banks of all the major industrial nations. In so far as they set targets in specific, numerical, terms, the average is always more than 1 per cent. For example, Bank of England (until 2003): 2.5 per cent (RPIX index; approximately 1.75 per cent, on average, in HICP terms); Sveriges Riksbank: 2±1 per cent (CPI); Norges Bank: 2.5±1 per cent (CPI); Bank of Canada: 1–3 per cent (CPI); Bank of Australia: 1–3 per cent (CPI); Reserve Bank of New Zealand: 1–3 per cent (CPI). The US Federal Reserve System and the Bank of Japan do not set their price stability targets in quantitative terms. The Swiss National Bank has decided on a definition of price stability that resembles that of the ECB. See the background study by Castelnuovo et al. (2003).

the HICP, as a new index, appears to have only a minimal measurement bias, that bias cannot be quantified with complete precision. In addition, this measurement bias may well diminish further as a result of additional improvements to Eurostat's calculation of the HICP (see Camba-Méndez, 2003; Wynne and Rodríguez-Palenzuela, 2002).

A further argument relates back to Akerlof, Dickens and Perry (1996), who claimed that a positive rate of inflation may support the necessary adjustment of relative prices to economic shocks where wages and prices are subject to downward nominal rigidities (see also Card and Hyslop, 1997). That said, empirical evidence indicates that price and wage rigidities depend fundamentally on confidence in the continuity of price stability and could therefore diminish with the transition to a low-inflation environment.[4] More recent studies by Cogley and Sargent (2001) and Brainard and Perry (2000) show that inflation in the United States has become less persistent over the last few years in the context of continuous price stability. Nominal rigidities cannot therefore be regarded as invariable structural features of an economy. Moreover, the purpose of monetary policy should hardly be to help accommodate or reinforce nominal rigidities by means of the conscious targeting of a higher rate of inflation (see Coenen, 2003a and 2003b).

Inflation differentials brought about by the Balassa-Samuelson effect discussed above (Balassa, 1964; Samuelson, 1964) are often cited as another reason for seeking, by means of monetary policy, to achieve a positive rate of inflation. Otherwise, the possible exist-

---

4   See also Benati (2003), which examines time series from the period of the gold standard.

ence of downward rigidities in prices and wages in the euro area could give rise to excessive costs in countries and regions with lower than average inflation over the longer term (see Rodríguez-Palenzuela, Camba-Méndez and García, 2003). As indicated above, monetary policy should not reinforce such market rigidities. Moreover, a number of empirical studies have found that the average rate of inflation in countries with a lower rate of price increases, resulting from the Balassa-Samuelson effect, will be at most half a percentage point lower than the euro area average.[5] Looking forward to the potential enlargement of the euro area, the overall impact of the Balassa-Samuelson effect should still remain limited. This is due not only to the fact that the economies of the acceding countries are relatively small, but also to the fact that, by meeting the convergence criteria, these countries will presumably establish the conditions necessary for achieving low rates of inflation in the longer term.

On the whole, inflation differentials within a currency union are a normal element of adjustment to regional supply and demand factors. The Balassa-Samuelson effect is an equilibrium phenomenon that does not, in principle, require economic correction. Moreover, looking at the currency area as a whole, it appears unlikely that a particular region would experience falling prices in the longer term. That would create a more favourable relationship between this region and others in terms of prices, stimulating demand for the goods and services of the region in question and

---

5   Empirical studies of the Balassa-Samuelson effect overwhelmingly suggest that if the average rate of inflation within the euro area were, for example, 1.5 per cent, that would imply that the average rate of inflation in those countries with lower rates of price increases resulting from the impact of the Balassa-Samuelson effect would be very close to 1 per cent. See Rodríguez-Palenzuela, Camba-Méndez and García (2003).

thereby countering the downward pressure on prices. There is therefore no significant risk of prices falling in absolute terms in a specific region or country in a currency union in the longer term, provided that monetary policy successfully prevents situations in which deflationary risks exist for the currency area as a whole.

Clarification of the definition of price stability

These considerations suggest that the inflation rate must, on the one hand, be low enough to minimise the costs of inflation. On the other hand it should also provide a sufficient safety margin in order to successfully counter persistent deflationary risks arising as a result of destabilising expectations. The definition, in 1998, of price stability as an increase in the HICP for the euro area as a whole of below 2 per cent was consistent with these considerations. In May 2003 the Governing Council helped to clarify the definition of price stability, declaring that its monetary policy would target an inflation rate 'below, but close to, 2%' (ECB, 2003a and 2003b).

The two pillars of the strategy
Aims of the strategy

The strategy had to provide a sound and systematic framework for conducting internal analysis and decision-making, and also for communicating to the public the decisions taken on the basis of this framework. In devising the format and features of this strategy it seemed essential – not least given the ECB's special position as a new institution – to observe a number of principles. As a framework for internal analysis and decision-making, the strategy had to ensure systematic and efficient use of all relevant information. This required the use of a comprehensive set of information based on a diverse range of approaches and models in order to obtain a comprehensive picture of the state of the economy and the risks to price stability. As, in the Governing Council's view, transparency means ensuring that the content of external communication is in line with internal analysis and decision-making, the same framework was also to be used for communicating with the general public.

A price-stability-oriented policy must always take account of the nature and size of economic shocks, from which risks to price stability can emerge, and of the way in which these shocks – given the potential reaction of monetary policy – affect the expectations of economic agents. Above all, transparency means giving an open and frank account of the analysis underlying monetary policy decisions in order to promote a sound understanding among the markets and the public of how a central bank conducts its monetary policy.

The two-pillar approach

In this vein, the Governing Council's strategy review also confirmed the two-pillar approach. As before, the assessment of the risks to price stability encompasses an economic and a monetary analysis, i.e. two complementary perspectives (ECB, 2003a, 2003b; ECB, 1998, 1999, 2000b). In order to better reflect this approach to the assessment of the risks to price stability, the Governing Council restructured both the president's introductory statement to the press conference that follows the first Governing Council meeting of the month and the editorial of the ECB's *Monthly Bulletin*. In addition, given the medium-to-long-term nature of the reference value for monetary growth, the Governing Council decided that it would no longer be reviewed on an annual basis.

Economic analysis

The *economic analysis* focuses mainly on the assessment of current economic and financial developments from the perspective of the interplay between supply and demand in the goods, services and factor markets. This includes financial developments, which provide information on households' and corporations' financial and net wealth positions as relevant factors shaping consumption and investment choices. In this respect, the macroeconomic projections serve to structure and synthesise a large amount of economic data. Despite this, they are not – for reasons elaborated below – an all-encompassing tool for the conduct of monetary policy.

Monetary analysis

The *monetary analysis* serves as a means of cross-checking, from a medium-to-long-term perspective, the short-to-medium-term indications arising from the economic analysis. In October 1998 the Governing Council assigned a prominent role to money in recognition of the fact that, in the medium to long run, monetary growth and inflation are closely related and in order to have at its disposal a reliable nominal indicator providing key information at time horizons stretching beyond those usually adopted for the construction of central bank inflation projections.

Thorough analysis of the specific situation – i.e. the particular degree of uncertainty referred to above and, in particular, the risk of structural breaks in well-established macroeconomic relationships, as induced by the regime shift of monetary union – clearly revealed that a strategy of monetary targeting was not appropriate. Furthermore, short-term monetary developments can also be driven by marked money demand shocks which are not linked with medium-term price trends that give rise to fluctuations in monetary aggregates that do not imply likely corresponding fluctuations in the price level. This is why the Governing Council decided against monetary targeting in 1998 and also stuck to this decision in 2003.

The prominent role assigned to money in the ECB's strategy is signalled by the announcement of a reference value for monetary growth. The reference value represents a public commitment to thoroughly analysing monetary developments and ensuring that information on monetary developments is given appropriate weight in the decision-making process. It specifies the growth rate of money regarded as consistent with price stability over the medium term. The monetary aggregate used to define the reference value should therefore exhibit a stable (or at least predictable) relationship with the price level. In the euro area, the broad aggregate M3 satisfies this criterion, as shown by numerous money demand studies.[6] The reference value has not been defined over short horizons – such as a year – and is altered only when there are reasons to assume that there has been a change to fundamental factors affecting the relationship between developments in M3 and price stability over the medium term. Prolonged and/or substantial deviations of monetary growth from the reference

6   See, for example, Coenen and Vega (2001); Brand and Cassola (2004); and Calza, Gerdesmeier and Levy (2001).

value should, under normal circumstances, signal risks to price stability.

The comprehensive analysis of the liquidity situation in terms of the monetary pillar goes far beyond an assessment of monetary growth in relation to the reference value. From the outset, the Governing Council has consistently emphasised the medium-term character of the monetary perspective and stressed that there is no direct link between short-term monetary developments and monetary policy decisions. Furthermore, in May 2003 the Governing Council also decided that it would no longer conduct a review of the reference value on an annual basis. This may help to dispel the occasional misperception that the reference value applies specifically to the year ahead. In maintaining its two-pillar strategy, the ECB also underscored the fact that its monetary policy is conducted from a medium-term perspective in order to preclude excessive policy activism and overly ambitious attempts to fine-tune economic developments.

Inflation targeting

In 1998 the ECB also discussed a strategy of direct inflation targeting as a particularly relevant option. In its strategy review the Governing Council again looked closely at the pertinent arguments.

In the last two decades many countries have moved to a stability-oriented monetary policy framework. As a result, central banks have made a credible commitment to targeting low and stable inflation rates. In this context, a number of central banks have chosen a strategy of inflation targeting. Essentially, this encompasses the following:

- Price stability as the primary objective.
- The public announcement of an inflation rate to be maintained over a more or less precisely defined time horizon.
- Transparency of the monetary policy strategy through appropriate communication with the markets and the public on monetary policy decisions.
- Greater accountability on the part of the central bank as regards the fulfilment of its mandate.

In retrospect, the policies pursued within this framework can doubtless be said to have been a great success in terms of achieving price stability. Particularly in countries which, starting from a relatively high level of inflation, announced a disinflation process, inflation targets were a suitable means of bringing inflation expectations into line with the objective of the monetary authorities.

These features of inflation targeting characterise nearly all stability-oriented central banks. In this general sense, Ben Bernanke (2003) has even described the Deutsche Bundesbank as a 'prototype inflation targeter'. Much the same could be said of the ECB. Normally, however, inflation targeting is also defined as a strategy in which macroeconomic forecasts – in particular for the inflation rate – serve as an intermediate target, i.e. as the primary or even all-encompassing variable for monetary policy decision-making and external communication (Svensson, 1997; 1999: 623). In this respect, inflation targeting can be understood as inflation forecast targeting.

The ECB quite consciously dismissed this strategy, and for good reason (see Issing, 2003). I should like to briefly explain the main considerations which informed this decision. The use of inflation forecasts as an intermediate target has mostly taken the form of a procedure whereby a central bank selects, from among a range of simulated alternatives, the key interest rate path for which expected inflation *at a certain point in the future* coincides with the inflation target (Svensson, 1999; Bowen, 1995: 57). Such focus on a fixed horizon does not seem robust; nor would it appear optimal from a welfare perspective. The horizon over which to pursue price stability is to a substantial degree contingent on the size and nature of shocks affecting the economy, as well as on the initial state of the economy. For example, to maintain the same degree of volatility of inflation and output, monetary policy can compensate for demand shocks over shorter periods than supply shocks as the latter move inflation and output in opposite directions and have to be addressed in a different way from demand shocks. Furthermore, the approach of inflation targeting ignores the implications that an interest rate path simulated in this way may have for price stability at longer horizons. In particular, it ignores the fact that – for a given interest rate path – the longer the horizon, the further the inflation rate can deviate from the target.

In addition, the construction and publication of central bank forecasts can raise a whole number of problems which severely limit the relevance of such forecasts for monetary policy. One of the main problems lies in constructing a forecast that is consistent with the underlying interest rate path. Exogenous assumptions with regard to the interest rate path – such as assuming constant interest rates – typically lead (especially in the case of forward-looking models) to instabilities or indeterminacy (Woodford, 2000). At the same time, bringing exogenous assumptions on the interest rate policy into line with the expectations of economic agents underlying these forecasts in a credible and convincing way in practice constitutes a considerable challenge. The aforementioned simulation of alternative interest rate paths is thus barely practicable. An alternative to this would be to use market interest rates, as opposed to a fixed interest rate. If the central bank's reaction function is understood by the public and the markets, and if its monetary policy enjoys credibility, the interest rate path expected by the market will mostly be consistent with the envisaged inflation target. If further economic shocks arise, however, it can be extremely difficult to communicate necessary deviations of the monetary policy stance from the interest rate path anticipated in this way. This can place an undue restriction on the ability of monetary policy to react in a timely manner to changes in economic conditions and in risks to price stability.

Last but not least, inflation forecast targeting neglects the information stemming from monetary developments. Up to now it has not proved possible to integrate the monetary side into the inflation forecast in a satisfactory manner. Whether this will ever be possible in a convincing way – not least on account of the different horizons involved – remains a matter of conjecture. At any rate, the Governing Council is adhering to its stance of considering *all* important indicators and of according monetary factors a prominent position in its assessment of the risks to price developments and thus in its monetary policy.

Medium-term orientation and the role of money

For good reason the ECB has chosen a strategy that does not focus exclusively on either a single indicator or a single analytical tool – be it money or an inflation forecast. By contrast, the two pillars of the ECB's strategy offer an appropriate means of bringing together and comparing different analytical perspectives and of using all the information relevant to decision-making in a systematic way. The advantages of this approach are increasingly being recognised, not least from the perspective of the relationship between monetary and credit developments and asset prices. As a result of the potential effects that share price booms – such as those witnessed in the 1990s – and their subsequent collapse may have on the financial system, the question of whether inflation targeting strategies are optimal in such an environment has recently attracted much attention (Bean, 2003). If financial imbalances accumulate and there is, for example, a sharp, broadly based increase in asset prices, there is little sense in continuing to pursue an inflation forecast for consumer prices over a horizon of one to two years. In such circumstances it may instead be advisable to set interest rates with a view to a time frame extending well beyond conventional forecast horizons – for example, in the face of substantial uncertainty about the sustainability of asset price movements (Kent and Lowe, 1997; Bordo and Jeanne, 2002). With the two pillars and medium-term orientation of its strategy, the ECB pays due attention to the need to take into account the entire horizon over which monetary policy impacts on the state of the economy (Issing, 2003).

Here the pre-emptive role of the monetary pillar of the strategy has also been acknowledged (Borio, English and Filardo, 2003). Growth rates of money and credit that are persistently in excess of those needed to sustain economic growth at non-inflationary levels may, under certain circumstances, provide early information on emerging financial instability. Such information is of relevance for monetary policy because the emergence of asset price bubbles could have a destabilising effect on activity and, ultimately, prices in the medium and longer term (Borio and Lowe, 2002; Masuch et al., 2003).

A number of observers have argued *against* using money as a monetary policy indicator. Some have argued, for example, that money loses its leading indicator properties in an environment of low inflation (see Begg et al., 2002) or that the long-term relationship between money and prices has been distorted on account of the regime shift associated with monetary union. A range of euro area studies carried out both within and outside the ECB, however, shows that there is no convincing reason to question the long-term relationship between money and inflation, not even in a low-inflation environment.[7] The sustained stability of money demand demonstrates that the long-term relationship between money and prices has remained intact following the introduction of the single currency (Bruggeman, Donati and Warne, 2003). There is little evidence to suggest that the relative attractiveness of holding instruments included in M3 as opposed to other financial instruments has been fundamentally altered as a result of structural changes in recent years (Calza and Sousa, 2003). Of course, no one can predict what course developments will take in the future. The current effects of financial market volatility and past declines in share prices require ongoing analysis of the appropriate definition of money and its stability properties. This means not only using

---

7   See Jaeger (2003); Gerlach (2003); Nicoletti Altimari (2001); Gerlach and Svensson (2004); Trecroci and Vega (2000). A number of observers have called for a strengthening of the role of money and the reference value; see von Hagen and Brückner (2001); Hayo, Neumann and von Hagen (1998). In addition, various monetary indicators can offer additional information on other macroeconomic variables, which may impact on price developments in due course. For example, narrow monetary aggregates have leading indicator properties for cyclical developments. See Brand, Seitz and Reimers (2003); Nelson (2002); Meltzer (1999).

the appropriate statistical instruments but also using the Eurosystem's detailed knowledge of the institutional features of the euro area's financial and monetary sector.

4 MONETARY POLICY INSTRUMENTS

Just as the treaty establishing the European Community did not provide a precise definition of the ECB's price stability mandate, so it was also left to the ECB to decide on the monetary policy instruments necessary for the operational framework. Both the operational framework and the strategy play a special role in the conduct of monetary policy. The strategy provides the basis for monetary policy decisions, which are geared towards maintaining price stability. The operational framework is used to implement this strategy in a consistent manner. The monetary policy instruments are listed in Table 1.

The ECB has chosen a set of instruments that is both simple and efficient (see Table 1). The open market operations and standing facilities serve to steer short-term money market interest rates and limit interest rate volatility. The marginal lending facility and deposit facility define the corridor within which the overnight rate can fluctuate (see Figure 4).[1] In addition, the ECB

---

1   The interest rate on the marginal lending facility is normally substantially higher than the corresponding market rate, and the interest rate on the deposit facility is normally substantially lower than the market rate. As a result, counterparties (credit institutions admitted to participate in the regular open market operations) normally only use the standing facilities when there are no alternatives. Since – except for the collateral requirements of the marginal lending facility – there are no limits on the access to these facilities, their interest rates normally provide a ceiling and a floor for the overnight rate in the money market (see also ECB, 2004: 84–5).

Table 1 **Monetary policy instruments**

Open market operations	• Weekly main refinancing operations • Monthly longer-term refinancing operations • Fine-tuning operations • Structural operations
Standing facilities	• Marginal lending facility • Deposit facility
Minimum reserve system	• 2 per cent ratio applied on deposits and debt securities with maturity up to two years and on money market papers • Remuneration • Averaging provision

requires credit institutions to hold minimum reserves on accounts with the European System of Central Banks (ESCB) in relation to their reserve base. Their most important function is to stabilise money market rates through the averaging provision mechanism[2] and increase the demand for central bank money by creating or enlarging a structural liquidity shortage in the market. In addition, the market-oriented remuneration of minimum reserves prevents the distortion of banks' international competitiveness and precludes evasive operations related to the requirement to hold minimum reserves (for further details see ECB, 2004: 77–90). In our experience, these monetary policy instruments have proved to be exceptionally robust.

Some adjustments have been made over time in response to periods of tension when pronounced speculation on an imminent

---

2   In order to meet their minimum reserve requirements, credit institutions have to hold balances on their current accounts with the national central banks. Thereby, compliance with reserve requirements is determined on the basis of the average of the daily balances on the credit institutions' reserve accounts over the reserve maintenance period of around one month.

Figure 4   **Key ECB interest rates and the EONIA (%)**

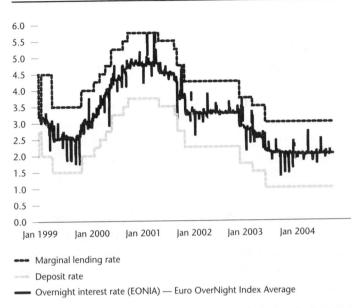

●■● Marginal lending rate

▫▫▫ Deposit rate

━━ Overnight interest rate (EONIA) — Euro OverNight Index Average

interest rate change has affected counterparties' bidding in the main refinancing operations. On several occasions, when expectations were high that the key ECB interest rates were about to be increased, counterparties submitted increasingly excessive bids in the main refinancing operations (leading to what is known as 'overbidding'). Similarly, expectations of an imminent reduction in the key ECB rates on occasion led counterparties to submit bids that on aggregate fell short of the amount needed to ensure that the reserve requirements were met ('underbidding').

Both problems stemmed mainly from the fact that the timing of the reserve maintenance periods was independent of the dates of the Governing Council meetings at which changes to the key ECB rates were decided. Thus changes to the key ECB interest rates could occur within the maintenance period. In addition, the maturity of the weekly main refinancing operations (which was two weeks) was such that at least the last operation of each reserve maintenance period overlapped with the subsequent reserve maintenance period. As a result, bidding behaviour in the main refinancing operations conducted at the end of a maintenance period could be affected by expectations of changes in the key ECB interest rates in the next reserve maintenance period.

To respond to this problem the Governing Council decided on two measures that have been effective as of March 2004: first, the timing of reserve maintenance periods was adjusted so that the periods always start on the settlement day of the main refinancing operation following the Governing Council meeting at which the monthly assessment of the monetary policy stance is pre-scheduled. This direct relationship between the Governing Council meeting and the start of the reserve maintenance period aims at ensuring that, as a rule, there are no expectations of changes to the key ECB rates occurring during the reserve maintenance period. Second, the maturity of the main refinancing operations was shortened from two weeks to one, aiming at eliminating the spillover of interest rate speculation from one reserve maintenance period to the next. The objective of the two combined measures was to contribute towards stabilising the conditions under which counterparties bid in the main refinancing operations.

These adjustments have left the salient features of the operational framework unaffected: the operational framework continues to rely on self-regulating market mechanisms and the

ECB's limited presence in the open market. The ECB has been able to steer liquidity and interest rates in a smooth manner and so, by stabilising money market rates, ensure the transmission of monetary policy impulses to the whole economy. This success reflects the high degree of credibility surrounding its operational potential and ability to manage liquidity. In addition, these tools have shown that the ECB's monetary policy is highly adaptable to a changing financial and economic environment. This was particularly evident in the fact that, while many central banks around the world had to implement extensive measures in preparation for the millennium changeover, the Eurosystem was able to use its existing instruments.

5 TRANSPARENCY AND ACCOUNTABILITY

The Maastricht Treaty clearly assigns to the Eurosystem the responsibility for the maintenance of price stability, and it has granted the ECB full political independence in its pursuit of this goal. The independence of the ECB and the need for transparency and accountability go hand in hand. Given the European nature of its mandate to maintain price stability and its independent status, the ECB is accountable to the European public and its elected representatives. This requires transparency in all areas relevant to the fulfilment of its mandate and a willingness to convey to the public, in a systematic and consistent way, all information relevant to its decision-making. Transparency is also essential to the effectiveness and success of the ECB's monetary policy. It should contribute to the anchoring of inflation expectations and minimise false expectations on the part of financial markets and the wider public regarding policy responses. For these reasons, the monetary policy strategy has been a key device. It clearly specifies how the ECB's policy objective is to be understood. And it provides a clear and coherent framework for structuring information and the decision-making process internally and explaining the ECB's policy stance to the general public.

Given the complexity of the real world and the permanent changes to the structural relationships underlying the economic system, it is presumably uncontroversial to state that the full specification of a policy rule or complete transparency as regards the underlying information set is impracticable. Where communication with the public is concerned, it must be acknowledged that a high degree of disclosure does not necessarily mean greater transparency (Poole, 2003; Issing, 1999). There is clearly a need to strike a balance between, on the one hand, being clear enough to be properly understood by the general public and, on the other, providing information that is sufficiently comprehensive to do justice to the uncertainties and complexity of the decision-making process. In fact, it has been a particular challenge to achieve clarity in our communication – i.e. to send clear, coherent and consistent messages to the markets and the wider public, thereby preventing misunderstanding and false expectations.

The regular publication of the Governing Council's assessment of the economic situation and the associated risks to price stability is an important part of our pursuit of transparency. Monetary policy decisions are regularly explained at the press conference that takes place immediately after the first Governing Council meeting of the month. Further details are presented in the ECB's *Monthly Bulletin*, in the speeches given by members of the Governing Council and in the president's testimonies before the European Parliament. With its monthly press conference, the ECB was the first central bank to provide such extensive and open real-time diagnosis – and other central banks are now moving in the same direction. The ongoing explanation of policy decisions and the details of the assessment on which these decisions are based seeks to enhance the public's understanding of the evolution of key ECB interest rates in response to economic shocks over time.

6 THE CONDUCT OF MONETARY POLICY: THE EXPERIENCE OF THE FIRST FIVE YEARS

What is the ECB's track record as regards the implementation of monetary policy over a little more than five years? How successful has the ECB's strategy been as a monetary policy framework for reacting to economic shocks in a way that ensures that price stability is maintained over the medium term?

One of the features that dominated the early years of European monetary policy was the existence of substantial and prolonged upward price shocks between the second half of 1999 and 2001. Initially the strongest impact came from a sharp increase in oil prices in conjunction with a general rise in import prices, reflecting exchange rate and global price developments. By the end of 2000 oil and import prices had risen to levels unseen since the beginning of the 1990s. While this trend reversed in 2001, the food price component of the HICP rose considerably because of livestock diseases. These were the main reasons why year-on-year inflation rose to more than 3 per cent in May 2001.

These factors were naturally beyond the ECB's control. In this context, and also on account of the robust economic growth witnessed in 1999 and 2000, the still-booming stock markets and the continued accumulation of excess liquidity, the Governing Council progressively increased the interest rates on the main refinancing operations by 225 basis points between November 1999 and October 2000 with the aim of maintaining price stability in the medium term. In particular, the aim was to prevent the shocks in question from affecting medium-to-long-term euro area inflation expectations.

Despite the prolonged impact of sharply rising food prices, it emerged in 2001 that, on account of weakening demand and the gradual reversal of monetary trends, lower interest rates were required in order to maintain price stability over the medium term. Accordingly, the Governing Council decided to lower interest rates from the spring of 2001 onward. In so doing, it reacted in a timely fashion to a number of negative demand shocks that later continued in the context of global uncertainties (such as those related to the terrorist attacks on 11 September 2001 and the wars in Afghanistan and Iraq). Since June 2003 the Governing Council has kept interest rates steady, with the minimum bid rate on the main refinancing operations remaining at the historically low level of 2 per cent.

Since the second half of 2003 the prospects for a gradual economic recovery have brightened following the end of the war in Iraq and as a result of the normalisation of financial market conditions, strengthening economic confidence, a recovery in global demand and ongoing increases in productivity and profitability in the corporate sector. As a consequence, however, of rather weak increases in productivity, adverse food price developments and higher oil prices – although the latter were attenuated by the appreciation of the euro – it was only in early 2004 that inflation fell below the upper ceiling of 2 per cent laid down in the definition of price stability.

Whenever it has been confronted with new economic conditions, the Governing Council of the ECB has not hesitated to take resolute action to pursue a policy that best serves the purpose of

Figure 5   **HICP inflation and key ECB interest rates (%)**

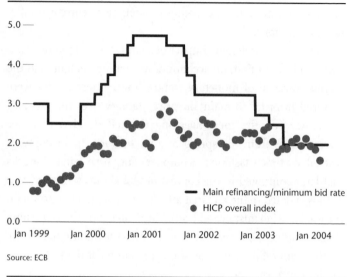

Source: ECB

maintaining price stability in the medium term. In line with the medium-term orientation of the ECB's monetary policy, interest rate adjustments in response to adverse economic shocks have generally been made gradually, thereby avoiding frequent shifts in the ECB's policy stance. This non-activist policy has contributed strongly to stabilising medium-term interest rate expectations at the level appropriate to the circumstances. It has also ensured that, in the face of strong share price fluctuations resulting from the initial new-economy euphoria and the subsequent disillusionment, monetary policy has not itself become a source of destabilising expectations. This has helped to anchor long-term inflation expectations at levels consistent with price stability. The medium-term perspective of the ECB's policy is also signalled by the fact that the Governing Council decided to lower interest rates in May 2001 – i.e. at a time when consumer price inflation had just peaked (see Figure 5) and real growth rates for the previous few quarters were still robust.

Since June 2003 the Governing Council has kept interest rates steady, with the minimum bid rate on the main refinancing operations thus remaining at the historically low level of 2 per cent. This is the lowest level of interest rates seen in Europe since World War II.

Did the monetary policy strategy prove to be a success in the first five years of its existence? Has confidence in the ECB's ability to fulfil its mandate strengthened? Of course, one measure would be to look at developments in the HICP. In fact, the average annual increase in the HICP over the first five years was slightly below 2 per cent, despite substantial adverse price shocks that occurred during this time. Another measure of the ECB's success can be derived from developments in long-term interest rates, reflecting market expectations for long-term inflation risks. For example, developments in French HICP-indexed bonds (see ECB, 2003b: 33) show that, since the beginning of monetary union, long-term inflation expectations have been anchored at levels consistent with the definition of price stability (see Figure 6). This is supported by the ECB's Survey of Professional Forecasters. This anchoring of inflation expectations has helped to promote the smooth functioning of monetary policy and can rightly be regarded as an indication of the high degree of credibility enjoyed by the ECB.

Communication between the ECB on the one hand and the financial markets and the general public on the other has – especially at the start of the single monetary policy – not always been without difficulties. It is clear, however, that communication

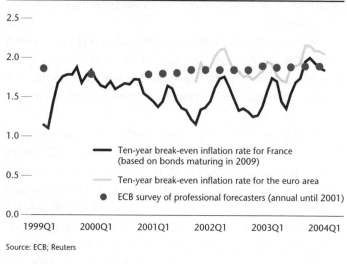

Figure 6   **Break-even inflation rate for French inflation-indexed bonds (monthly averages) and long-term inflation expectations on the basis of the ECB Survey of Professional Forecasters (%)**

Source: ECB; Reuters

between the ECB and both the public and the financial markets has improved considerably over time. So, too, has the public's understanding of the ECB's strategy. For example, some commentators initially confused the reference value with a monetary target; some assumed that the ECB was pursuing a monetary targeting strategy, while others implied that it was pursuing an inflation targeting strategy on the basis of an inflation forecast or even a mixture of both. Such misinterpretations have since become rare.

Since the ECB's inception the institutional framework for securing a stable European currency and lasting economic success has proved itself in practice. None of the fears mentioned above has materialised. For the benefits of a stable single currency to be reaped in full by all participating member states, however, a number of challenges have yet to be met. The ECB has emphasised time and again that the single monetary policy remains handicapped by the existence of considerable structural rigidities in the European Union. As much has been left undone in recent years, it is now more crucial than ever to implement structural reforms in order to improve the growth potential of the euro area economies. This would also strengthen their capacity for responding appropriately to macroeconomic shocks. Conditions in labour markets, in particular, fall far short of the criteria for optimum currency areas.

Since the introduction of the single currency, competition in the euro area has increased considerably. If the economic fundamentals of a particular euro area country are inferior to those of other regions of the euro area, this will have a direct and pronounced effect on its competitiveness. In any case, the euro area countries still have much to do in terms of progressing deregulation and increasing flexibility – not least in labour markets. The risks posed by structural growth weaknesses in a number of member states might give rise to a temptation to put pressure on monetary policy to address problems that it cannot solve – in particular, structural employment and growth deficiencies. This would hinder the success of monetary policy considerably. The same can be said of any undermining of the Stability and Growth Pact as a key element of the framework for monetary union. In view of the enlargement of the European Union, it is even more imperative that governments be mindful of their own particular responsibility and thereby help to ensure lasting prosperity.

REFERENCES

Akerlof, G. A., W. T. Dickens and G. L. Perry (1996), 'The macroeconomics of low inflation', *Brookings Papers on Economic Activity*, 1: 1–59

Alesina, A., O. Blanchard, J. Galì, F. Giavazzi and H. Uhlig (2001), 'Defining a macroeconomic framework for the euro area', *Monitoring the European Central Bank*, 3, London: CEPR

Angeloni, I. and M. Ehrmann (2003), 'Monetary policy transmission in the euro area: any changes after EMU?', ECB Working Paper no. 240

Angeloni I., A. Kashyap and B. Mojon (eds) (2003), *Monetary Policy Transmission in the Euro Area*, Cambridge University Press

Atkeson, A. and T. Bayoumi (1993), 'Do private markets insure against regional shocks in a common currency area? Evidence from the US', *Open Economies Review*, 4: 303–24

Balassa, B. (1964), 'The purchasing power parity doctrine: a reappraisal', *Journal of Political Economy*, 72: 584–96

Bayoumi, T. and B. Eichengreen (1993a), 'Shocking aspects of European monetary unification', in F. Giavazzi and F. Torres (eds), *Adjustment and Growth in the European Union*, Cambridge University Press, pp. 193–230

Bayoumi, T. and B. Eichengreen (1993b), 'Is there a conflict between EC enlargement and European Monetary Unification?', *Greek Economic Review*, 15: 131–54

Bean, C. (2003), 'Asset prices, financial imbalances and monetary policy: are inflation targets enough?', mimeo, BIS, March

Begg, D., F. Canova, P. de Grauwe, A. Fatás and P. Lane (2002), 'Surviving the slowdown', *Monitoring the European Central Bank*, 4, London: CEPR

Benati, L. (2003), 'Investigating inflation persistence across monetary regimes', forthcoming as a Bank of England Working Paper

Bernanke, B. S. (2003), 'A perspective on inflation targeting', speech delivered at the Annual Washington Policy Conference of the National Association of Business Economists, Washington, DC, 25 March

Beyer, A., J. A. Doornik and D. F. Hendry (2001), 'Constructing historical euro-zone data', *Economic Journal*, 111: 102–21

Blanchard, O. and L. Katz (1992), 'Regional evolutions', *Brookings Papers on Economic Activity*, 1: 1–75

Bordo, M. and O. Jeanne (2002), 'Inflation shocks and financial distress: an historical analysis', Federal Reserve Bank of St Louis, Working Paper Series, no. 2000-005A

Borio, C., B. English and A. Filardo (2003), 'A tale of two perspectives: old or new challenges for monetary policy?', BIS Working Paper no. 127

Borio, C. and P. Lowe (2002), 'Asset prices, financial and monetary stability: exploring the nexus', BIS Working Paper no. 114

Bowen, A. (1995), 'British experience with inflation targetry', in L. Leiderman and L. E. O. Svensson (eds), *Inflation Targets*, London: Centre of Economic Policy Research, pp. 53–68

Brainard, W. and G. Perry (2000), 'Making policy in a changing world', in G. Perry and J. Tobin (eds), *Economic Events, Ideas, and Policies: the 1960s and After*, Brookings Institution Press, pp. 43–82

Brand, C. and N. Cassola (2004), 'A money demand system for euro area M3', *Applied Economics*, forthcoming

Brand, C., D. Gerdesmeier and B. Roffia (2002), 'Estimating the trend in M3 income velocity underlying the reference value for monetary growth', ECB Occasional Paper no. 3

Brand, C., F. Seitz and H.-E. Reimers (2003), 'Narrow money and the business cycle: theoretical aspects and euro area evidence', in O. Issing (ed.), *Background Studies for the ECB's Evaluation of its Monetary Policy Strategy*, ECB, pp. 301–28

Bruggemann, A., P. Donati and A. Warne (2003), 'Is the demand for euro area M3 stable?', in O. Issing (ed.), *Background Studies for the ECB's Evaluation of its Monetary Policy Strategy*, ECB, pp. 245–300

Calza, A., D. Gerdesmeier and J. Levy (2001), 'Euro area money demand: measuring the opportunity costs appropriately', IMF Working Paper no. 01/179

Calza, A. and J. Sousa (2003), 'Why has money demand been more stable in the euro area than in other economies? A literature review', in O. Issing (ed.), *Background Studies for the ECB's Evaluation of its Monetary Policy Strategy*, ECB, pp. 229–44

Camba-Méndez, G. (2003), 'The definition of price stability: choosing a price measure', in O. Issing (ed.), *Background*

Studies for the ECB's Evaluation of its Monetary Policy Strategy, ECB, pp. 31–42

Card, D. and D. Hyslop (1997), 'Does inflation "grease the wheels" of the labor market?', NBER Working Paper no. 5538

Castelnuovo, E., S. Nicoletti Altimari and D. Rodríguez-Palenzuela (2003), 'Definition of price stability, range and point inflation targets: the anchoring of long-term inflation expectations', in O. Issing (ed.), *Background Studies for the ECB's Evaluation of its Monetary Policy Strategy*, ECB, pp. 43–90

Coenen, G. (2003a), 'Zero lower bound: is it a problem in the euro area?', in O. Issing (ed.), *Background Studies for the ECB's Evaluation of its Monetary Policy Strategy*, ECB, pp. 139–56

Coenen, G. (2003b), 'Downward nominal wage rigidity and the long-run Phillips curve: simulation-based evidence for the euro area', in O. Issing (ed.), *Background Studies for the ECB's Evaluation of its Monetary Policy Strategy*, ECB, pp. 127–38

Coenen, G. and J.-L. Vega (2001), 'The demand for M3 in the euro area', *Journal of Applied Econometrics*, 16: 727–48

Cogley, T. and T. J. Sargent (2001), 'Evolving post-WWII US inflation dynamics', in B. Bernanke and K. Rogoff (eds), *NBER Macroeconomics Annual 2001*, Cambridge, MA: MIT Press, pp. 331–7

De Grauwe, P. (2002), *Economics of Monetary Union*, Oxford University Press, 5th edn, ch. 8.

Dotsey, M. and P. Ireland (1996), 'The welfare costs of inflation in general equilibrium', *Journal of Monetary Economics*, 45: 631–55

ECB (1998), *A Stability-Oriented Monetary Policy Strategy for the ESCB*, press release, 13 October, www.ecb.int/press/pr981013_1.htm

ECB (1999), 'The stability-oriented monetary policy of the Eurosystem', *Monthly Bulletin*, January, pp. 39–50

ECB (2000a), 'The switch to variable rate tenders in the main refinancing operations', *Monthly Bulletin*, July, pp. 37–42

ECB (2000b), 'The two pillars of the ECB's monetary policy strategy', *Monthly Bulletin*, November, pp. 37–48

ECB (2001), *Why Price Stability?*, 1st ECB Central Banking Conference, November 2000, www.ecb.int/home/conf/cbc1/cbc1.htm

ECB (2003a), *The ECB's Monetary Policy Strategy*, press release, 8 May, www.ecb.int/press/03/pr030508_2en.htm

ECB (2003b), 'The outcome of the ECB's evaluation of its monetary policy strategy', *Monthly Bulletin*, June, pp. 79–92

ECB (2003c), 'Changes to the Eurosystem's operational framework for monetary policy', *Monthly Bulletin*, August, pp. 41–54

ECB (2003d), *Inflation Differentials in the Euro Area: Potential Causes and Policy Implications*, September, www.ecb.int/pub/pdf/other/inflationdifferentialreporten.pdf

ECB (2004), *The Monetary Policy of the ECB*, Frankfurt: European Central Bank, www.ecb.int/pub/pdf/monetarypolicy2001.pdf

European Economic Advisory Group (2003), *Report on the European Economy 2003*

Fagan, G., J. Henry and R. Mestre (2001), 'An area-wide model (AWM) for the euro area', ECB Working Paper no. 42

Feldstein, M. (1997), 'The costs and benefits of going from low inflation to price stability', in C. Romer and D. Romer (eds), *Reducing Inflation: Motivation and Strategy*, University of Chicago Press, pp. 136–56

Feldstein, M. (1999), *The Costs and Benefits of Price Stability*, University of Chicago Press for NBER

Fischer, S. (1981), 'Towards an understanding of the costs of inflation', II, Carnegie-Rochester Conference Series on Public Policy, 15: 5–41

Fitoussi, J.-P. and J. Creel (2002), *How to Reform the European Central Bank*, London: Centre for European Reform

Friedman, M. (1968), 'The role of monetary policy', *American Economic Review*, 58: 1–17

Gerlach, S. (2003), 'The ECB's two pillars', CEPR Discussion Paper no. 3689

Gerlach, S. and L. E. O. Svensson (2004), 'Money and inflation in the euro area: a case for monetary indicators?', *Journal of Monetary Economics*, 50: 1,649–72

Gros, D., J. Jimeno, C. Monticelli, G. Tabellini and N. Thygesen (2001), 'Testing the speed limit for Europe', Third Report of the CEPS Macroeconomic Policy Group

Hayo, B., M. J. M. Neumann and J. von Hagen (1998), 'A monetary target for the ECB?', EMU Monitor background paper, University of Bonn

IMF (2002), Concluding statement of the IMF mission on the economic policies of the euro area – in the context of the 2002 Article IV consultation discussions with the euro area countries, 12 July

Issing, O. (1998), 'Die Europäische Zentralbank – Das Problem der Glaubwürdigkeit', in D. Duwendag (ed.), *Finanzmärkte im*

Spannungsfeld von Globalisierung, Regulierung und Geldpolitik, Berlin: Schriften des Vereins für Socialpolitik, NF, 261: 179–92

Issing, O. (1999), 'The Eurosystem: transparent and accountable or "Willem in Euroland"', *Journal of Common Market Studies*, 37: 503–19

Issing, O. (2001), 'The single monetary policy of the European Central Bank: one size fits all', *International Finance*, 4: 441–62

Issing, O. (2002a), 'Monetary policy in a changing economic environment', *Federal Reserve Bank of Kansas City Economic Review*, 87: 15–36

Issing, O. (2002b), 'Monetary policy in a world of uncertainty', speech delivered at the Economic Policy Forum, Paris, www.ecb.int/key/02/sp021209.htm

Issing, O. (2003), 'Inflation targeting: a view from the ECB', speech delivered at the Federal Reserve Bank of St Louis symposium 'Inflation targeting: prospects and problems', 16–17 October, forthcoming in the *Federal Reserve Bank of St Louis Review*

Issing, O., V. Gaspar, I. Angeloni and O. Tristani (2001), *Monetary Policy in the Euro Area: Strategy and Decision-making at the European Central Bank*, Cambridge University Press

Jaeger, A. (2003), 'The ECB's money pillar: an assessment', IMF Working Paper WP/03/82

Kent, C. and P. Lowe (1997), 'Asset-price bubbles and monetary policy', Research Discussion Paper no. 9709, Reserve Bank of Australia

Klaeffling, M. and V. Lopez (2003), 'Inflation targets and the liquidity trap', in O. Issing (ed.), *Background Studies for the ECB's Evaluation of its Monetary Policy Strategy*, ECB, pp. 157–86

Lucas, R. E. (1976), 'Econometric policy evaluation: a critique',
    Carnegie-Rochester Conference Series on Public Policy, 1: 19–46

Lucas, R. E. (1981), 'Discussion of S. Fischer, towards an
    understanding of the costs of inflation', II, *Carnegie-Rochester
    Conference Series on Public Policy*, 15: 43–52

Masuch, K., S. Nicoletti Altimari, H. Pill and M. Rostagno
    (2003), 'The role of money in monetary policy making', in
    O. Issing (ed.), *Background Studies for the ECB's Evaluation of
    its Monetary Policy Strategy*, ECB, pp. 187–228

Meltzer, A. H. (1999), 'The transmission process', working paper,
    Carnegie Mellon University

Nelson, E. (2002), 'Direct effects of base money on aggregate
    demand', *Journal of Monetary Economics*, 49: 687–708

Nicoletti Altimari, S. (2001), 'Does money lead to inflation in the
    euro area?', ECB Working Paper no. 63

Orphanides, A. and W. Wieland (1998), 'Price stability and
    monetary policy effectiveness when nominal interest rates are
    bounded at zero', Finance and Economics Discussion Series
    no. 35, Federal Reserve Board, Washington, DC

Poole, W. (2003), 'Fed transparency: how, not whether', *Federal
    Reserve Bank of St Louis Review*, 85(6): 1–8

Reifschneider, D. and J. C. Williams (2000), 'Three lessons for
    monetary policy in a low inflation era', *Journal of Money,
    Credit and Banking*, pp. 936–66

Rodríguez-Palenzuela, D., G. Camba-Méndez and J. A. García
    (2003), 'Relevant economic issues concerning the optimal
    rate of inflation', in O. Issing (ed.), *Background Studies for the
    ECB's Evaluation of its Monetary Policy Strategy*, ECB, pp. 91–
    126

Rogers, J. H. (2001), 'Price level convergence, relative prices and inflation in Europe', International Finance Discussion Papers no. 699, Board of Governors of the Federal Reserve System

Sachverständigenrat zur Begutachtung der gesamtwirtschaftlichen Entwicklung (2002), *Jahresgutachten 2002/2003: Zwanzig Punkte für Beschäftigung und Wachstum*, Stuttgart

Samuelson, P. (1964), 'Theoretical notes on trade problems', *Review of Economics and Statistics*, 46: 1–60

Svensson, L. E. O. (1997), 'Inflation forecast targeting: implementing and monitoring inflation targets', *European Economic Review*, 41: 1,111–46

Svensson, L. E. O. (1999), 'Inflation targeting as a monetary policy rule', *Journal of Monetary Economics*, 43: 607–54

Svensson, L. E. O. (2002), 'A reform of the Eurosystem's monetary policy strategy is increasingly urgent', briefing paper for the Committee on Economic and Monetary Affairs of the European Parliament

Svensson, L. E. O. (2003), 'How should the Eurosystem reform its monetary strategy?', briefing paper for the quarterly testimony of the president of the European Central Bank before the Committee on Economic and Monetary Affairs of the European Parliament

Trecroci, C. and J.-L. Vega (2000), 'The information content of M3 for future inflation', ECB Working Paper no. 33, October

Von Hagen, J. and M. Brückner (2001), 'Monetary policy in unknown territory: the European Central Bank in the early years', ZEI Working Paper 2001/0018

Wynne, M. and D. Rodríguez-Palenzuela (2002), 'Measurement bias in the HICP: what do we know and what do we need to know?', ECB Working Paper no. 131

Woodford, M. (2000), 'Pitfalls of forward-looking monetary policy', *American Economic Review Papers and Proceedings*, 90: 100–4

Yates, A. (2002), 'Monetary policy and the zero bound to interest rates: a review', ECB Working Paper Series no. 190

COMMENTARY
David B. Smith[1]

Introduction

Professor Issing's Mais Lecture represents a lucid combination of high theory with the nuts-and-bolts practicality required to ensure that EMU got off the ground, and provided its passengers with a smooth ride, despite flying through turbulent world events. His presentation tactfully confines itself to the role of the ECB within the euro zone. Issing's views, however, are also relevant to Britain's disappointingly parochial debate on whether this country should participate in monetary union; a debate that has tended to generate more heat than light, and has also made for some rather strange bedfellows. One reason for the latter is that EMU cuts at right angles across many traditional intellectual boundaries. This is because it can be argued that monetary union from its conception was essentially a broad-money monetarist project on Bundesbank lines, but one that also impinged on the monetary independence of its member nations.

The ironic result has been that British left-of-centre, and Keynesian-inspired, economists have tended to be strongly in favour of UK participation in EMU for internationalist reasons

---

1   David Smith is Chief Economist at Williams de Broë and chairman of the IEA's Shadow Monetary Policy Committee.

– but would violently reject the monetarist-inspired economics that underlies it in a domestic context – while British monetarists have often been among the strongest opponents of UK participation because of the perceived threat that it posed to British sovereignty. The reason why these alignments appear strange in terms of economic theory is that it is the people who are most concerned that economies could get trapped in a permanent recession – in other words, old-school Keynesians – who should have been strongly opposed to the risks involved in Britain joining EMU. In contrast, Friedmanite monetarists, who believe that market economies have strong self-righting properties, might fear that signing up for EMU could engender an output shock in the short run, but should expect the real economy to be back on an even keel within five years or so. Finally, advocates of the rational-expectations approach should argue, if they are consistent, that even the transitional costs of EMU participation would be low, provided that the ECB had credible institutional arrangements which guaranteed that it would pursue sensible monetary policies.

The risk/reward argument

One good argument for not wanting to be a founder member of EMU in the 1990s was that, while the most likely scenario seemed benign, the risk/reward ratio was wrong because of the non-zero probability of a very bad outcome. This was because EMU arguably represented a slightly wild experiment, akin to looping the loop in an Airbus full of passengers. The role of Professor Issing and his ECB colleagues can then be regarded as being similar to that of highly skilled aircraft engineers, who successfully do all the right things to minimise the risks associated with this (not entirely reasonable) demand from their political masters. Christopher Wren's memorial in Saint Paul's Cathedral reads *Lector si monumentum requiris, circumspice* (Reader, if you seek his monument, look around you). Issing and his colleagues can take similar pride in the institutional artefact that they have constructed since the ECB was established on 1 June 1998. There must have been some serious concern in the early phase of EMU that the flight into the unknown represented by monetary union was an unjustified danger to the euro zone's 308 million passengers, because of the unprecedented nature of the experiment involved. It is also no secret that the Bundesbank had serious reservations about the viability of the EMU project in the early 1990s. Some of these concerns have abated. One issue that could still prove troublesome, however, is whether the ECB has the necessary legal powers to control the supplies of money and credit, and prevent the sort of moral hazard that gave rise to the US Savings and Loans fiasco in the 1980s, as long as legal authority resides with the individual euro zone states.

The twin pillars

Established central banks not only have the legal backing to enforce their will on the banking system, which is provided by a one-to-one correspondence between their geographic area of responsibility and the region over which the writ of their state applies, but also have access to long runs of historic economic data and can be fairly confident that the demands for money and credit will not be totally unstable. In its early years, neither of these last two conditions applied to the ECB for two reasons. The first was the dearth of usable aggregate euro zone statistics. This was not helped by the noticeable differences in the methods by which the existing economic statistics of the various individual euro zone economies were compiled, and their frequently poor quality and long compilation delays by Anglo-Saxon standards. There were also signs of a 'turf war' between Eurostat and the ECB at one point, as to which should be responsible for producing the long runs of pseudo back data for the euro zone required for statistical analysis.

The second risk involved in the EMU project was that the act of monetary union would itself destabilise the pan-European demand for money. This was because the new euro had noticeably different attributes from its predecessor currencies, for three reasons. The first was that it was a better medium of exchange, because it could be used over a wider area. The second reason was that the euro had different attributes when viewed as a store of value, because the inflation tax on money holdings was potentially reduced in the southern part of the euro zone, even if it may have risen in the northern part. The final and less-discussed reason why EMU could have destabilised the continent's demand for money is that EMU weakened the de facto local banking cartels in the individual euro zone states, which ultimately depended on the existence of separate national currencies to survive. These anti-competitive arrangements have been undermined by the increased transnational banking competition engendered by EMU, with the result that euro zone bank deposits have started to pay more competitive rates of interest. The increase in the 'own rate' paid on bank deposits seems to lead to a noticeable rise in the equilibrium ratio of broad money to national income in Britain after the more liberal Competition and Credit Control regime was introduced in the early 1970s. It is slightly surprising that it has not had a similar effect in continental Europe.

Meanwhile, Issing's account of how the ECB overcame the challenges associated with the unprecedented nature of the EMU experiment will help other central bankers operating in abnormally unstructured circumstances or setting up shop in new jurisdictions, such as the successor states to Yugoslavia.

The definition of price stability

One of the problems of much contemporary academic economics is that it is taught as a logically pure subject that does not attempt to mesh with the messy business of reality. This is unfortunate because the subject can become an empty intellectual game if the theoretical concepts employed by economists cannot be translated into quantified reflections of the real world. Thus, it is one thing to make out a general theoretical case in favour of price stability, and quite another to give it a precise operational definition in terms of a specific price index, which carries the trust of the mass of the citizenry. Issing's description of why the ECB decided to set an annual rate of increase of up to 2 per cent in the harmonised index of consumer prices (HICP) as its price target is particularly interesting for people in Britain, where both the original RPIX inflation target and its CPI successor (based on the HICP) were delivered by the Chancellor, Moses-like from on high, with almost no previous public discussion. Central bankers need to master both the theoretical and the intellectual issues and achieve workable and robust solutions in practice. The need to integrate theory and real-world implementation is one reason why central banking remains a fascinating art that stands quite independent of pure academic inquiry.

How the ECB differs from other central banks

A noteworthy aspect of Issing's paper is the way in which the ECB differs from other central banks, including the US Federal Reserve and the Bank of England, in both its theoretical approach and in its practices. Some of these reflect different institutional arrangements. There also seem to be genuine intellectual differences between the central banks, however, a lot of which appear to boil down to the perceived stability, or otherwise, of the demand for broad money. The demand-for-money relationship has had a crucial importance for monetarists ever since the mid-1950s when Milton Friedman replaced the earlier Irving Fisher view – that the ratio of money to income was some sort of technologically fixed constant – with the more sophisticated Cambridge approach, associated with people such as Alfred Marshall and Dennis Robertson. This claimed that the amount of real money balances society wanted to hold was a predictable function of a relatively small number of economic variables, such as real income, the level and structure of interest rates, and the inflation 'tax' on holding money balances. The demand-for-money relationship gave rise to a huge literature over several decades, and it was generally accepted that a stable equilibrium demand for money was a necessary, but not sufficient, condition for accepting the monetarist approach. Both the US Federal Reserve and the UK monetary authorities lost interest in money supply targets during the course of the 1980s because the relationship between money and the wider economy appeared to them to have broken down (although I would dispute this as a result of my own research for the UK). This alleged breakdown does not seem to have happened to anything like the same extent in Germany, and Professor Issing quotes ECB research suggesting that the demand for money has

Figure 7 **Annual percentage changes in OECD real GDP and OECD real broad money**

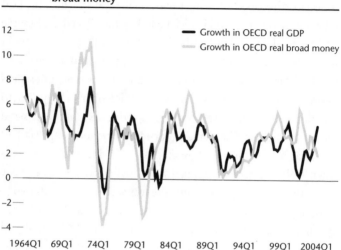

remained stable in the euro zone, despite the major institutional changes associated with monetary union.

The survival of a stable euro zone demand for money through the process of monetary union is superficially surprising, although some of it may reflect relatively subdued competition by Anglo-Saxon standards between deposit-taking institutions. There is also evidence to suggest, however, that the key monetarist relationships become stronger as one aggregates across countries, with the OECD area as a whole apparently behaving remarkably like a simple late-1950s Friedman model over the past four decades. In particular, there appear to be obvious links between the following variables: the growth of real broad-money balances and real GDP (see Figure 7) and the growth of nominal broad money in excess of

Figure 8   **Annual percentage changes in OECD 'excess' broad money and OECD consumer prices**

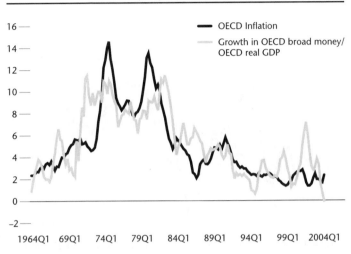

real output and consumer price inflation (see Figure 8). Also, there is a surprisingly stable ratio of broad money to nominal activity, albeit with a modest upward trend over time and some signs of an undigested spike of liquidity since 11 September 2001 (see Figure 9).

The increased stability of the core monetary relationships, which appears as the geographical area being investigated is widened, seems to be because three particular factors – which may be important for one country in isolation – are cancelled out at the level of the world as a whole. One is balance of payments surpluses and deficits: these imbalances weaken the link between money and inflation because individual countries can assuage excess demand by importing from abroad, for example, even if the

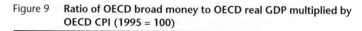

Figure 9   **Ratio of OECD broad money to OECD real GDP multiplied by OECD CPI (1995 = 100)**

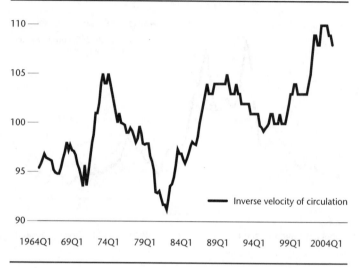

world as a whole cannot. The second factor that weakens the links between money and prices in open economies is abrupt shifts in the real exchange rate, such as the upward move in sterling that was observed after the autumn of 1996: these are relative movements, which have to be counterbalanced elsewhere, and therefore have no implications for the world as a whole. The final factor is the tendency for corporations and wealthy individuals to hold multi-currency asset portfolios: this can lead to weakened links between money and activity in any given country, but is again self-cancelling for the world as a whole. These considerations suggest that one reason why the demand for money may be more stable in the euro zone than in some individual European countries is that the share of international trade in the zone's GDP is only around one tenth. The euro zone may also be less affected by speculative moves between national monies than the UK, for example, because it lacks a global financial centre on a par with the City of London.

Controlling the supply of money

Because the ECB pays more attention to the course of broad money than other central banks, especially as an indicator of potential inflationary pressures beyond the reliable forecasting range of conventional predictive models, it also seems more concerned with the need to control money and credit than Anglo-Saxon central bankers, who generally have a more laissez-faire approach to their monetary sectors. In this respect, the ECB is following on from the Bundesbank, which often argued in the late 1980s that it was necessary to impose legally mandatory reserve asset requirements on the banking sector in order to control the supplies of broad money and credit. Indeed, the Bundesbank made it clear before Britain joined the ERM in 1990 that it regarded such arrangements as a necessary condition for participation in the ERM. This, together with the view that sterling had entered the system at too high a level, was the main reason why the Bundesbank was not prepared to assist the UK authorities when the pound came under pressure in September 1992. It might not be too late still to have a fruitful discussion of the case for mandatory reserve asset requirements in a British context, given the current rapid growth of broad money and credit in the UK, and the difficulties that seem to confront the Bank of England's Monetary Policy Committee (MPC) in its attempts to control the present British house price and borrowing booms.

The interface between fiscal and monetary policy

Professor Issing's paper concludes with a warning about the difficulty of maintaining monetary discipline when the labour market cannot clear because of an excessive regulatory burden and the economy's supply side is being undermined by excessive government spending, with the associated high tax burdens and large budget deficits.

In theory, the central bank can always control the level of nominal demand in the private sector of the economy through appropriate monetary policy actions. This may not be very helpful, however, where aggregate GDP is concerned, in a euro zone where general government outlays amounted to 48.9 per cent of the market-price measure of GDP in 2003, according to the latest OECD statistics. Furthermore, the technical problems facing the central bank get worse as the socialised sector of the economy expands. This is because closing any given GDP output gap requires forcing a coarser adjustment on the residual private sector. In addition, any particular monetary retrenchment is likely to take a greater toll on employment, because the 'natural' rate of unemployment (or NAIRU) is shifted outward as taxes and regulation increase. The political debate also tends to become more shrill as economic performance deteriorates, and opportunistic politicians start to blame the central bank for what are really the side effects of their own misguided policies.

Such tensions have long been apparent in the euro zone, and may even have been exacerbated by EMU. This is because it is easier for unscrupulous politicians to play the nationalist card and blame an allegedly 'foreign' institution, such as the ECB, for their own nation's economic difficulties. Britain's MPC did not have to bear the heat of this particular kitchen until recently, because the present government inherited a situation where Britain's tax burden was 8–9 percentage points lower than in the euro zone, and the labour market was far freer because of the reforms of the Thatcher years. Mr Blair's decision to sign up for the EU's Social Chapter, and the quite remarkable breakdown of fiscal discipline in recent years under the current Chancellor, suggest that Britain is now entering a period when the tensions between the governing politicians and the MPC are likely to escalate, because this would be the objective consequence of the policies now being pursued in our country.

Should Britain join EMU?

The analysis above suggests that there are limits on what can be achieved by monetary policy when profligate and interventionist politicians are slowly garrotting the economy's supply side in pursuit of their own sectional interests. Even so, there is evidence from international panel data studies – which combine time series and cross-section methods – that reducing both the rate of inflation and the volatility of inflation leads to superior economic growth. This means that well-conducted monetary policies have favourable real effects as well as delivering lower inflation. The first section of this commentary suggested that many of the popular economic reasons for opposing British participation in monetary union were invalid, particularly if one were a rational-expectations monetarist and accepted that Issing had made a strong case for believing that the ECB had a robust institutional structure and a strong commitment to fighting inflation.[2]

2   See also P. Schwartz, *The Euro as Politics*, Research Monograph 58, Institute of Economic Affairs, London, who argues this point.

One reason why one might still not want Britain to participate in EMU, even if one believed that the country would adjust eventually, would be the belief that the economic gains from membership would be so small that they would still be exceeded by the transitional adjustment costs. There is also the argument that a monetary policy tailor-made for a given country is always preferable to one that is conducted to satisfy the needs of a wider area, although this probably applies only in a world of less than full rational expectations, where economic disequilibria – such as high regional unemployment – can persist for a long time.

The real case against UK participation in monetary union is not that EMU has been, or will be, a disaster, or that one can permanently buy higher output and more jobs by debauching the currency. Rather, it is that the political realities mean that participation in EMU would inexorably lead to two further steps that would indeed do irrevocable, and possibly massive, damage to Britain's national interest. The first such step is that participation in EMU could lead to the acceptance of tax harmonisation and the full panoply of EU labour market interventions, something that would still be highly damaging to the real economy, even after the present government has thrown away so much of its golden inheritance. It is hard to see why any well-intentioned person would want to take a country such as Britain, with an employment rate of 74.7 per cent and an unemployment rate of 4.7 per cent, on standardised international definitions, and force upon it the tax and regulatory burdens that have left the euro zone with equivalent employment and jobless rates of 66.1 per cent and 9 per cent, respectively.

The second, and even more dangerous, step that might follow from British participation in EMU would be the adoption of the

European Constitution. This would destroy both Britain's entire common-law tradition, which underpins our liberties, and the legal basis for Britain's existence as a sovereign independent state. Whether Britain does eventually sign up for EMU presumably depends on political events and people's perceptions of the relative competence of the MPC and the ECB. Britain tends to huddle closer to the European project when its self-confidence is low, but look to the wide blue seas beyond when it is feeling bullish. One reason why the EMU debate has damped down in Britain in recent years is the widespread view that the MPC has done an excellent job since 1997, and that little is to be gained by handing our monetary policy over to others. This may change if the present house price boom leads to a hard landing, or the financial markets lose faith in Gordon Brown's feckless spending policies, and pull the rug from under sterling. In these situations, Britain might end up participating in EMU because it had once again lost faith in its ability to manage its own affairs.

ABOUT THE IEA

The Institute is a research and educational charity (No. CC 235 351), limited by guarantee. Its mission is to improve understanding of the fundamental institutions of a free society with particular reference to the role of markets in solving economic and social problems.

The IEA achieves its mission by:

- a high-quality publishing programme
- conferences, seminars, lectures and other events
- outreach to school and college students
- brokering media introductions and appearances

The IEA, which was established in 1955 by the late Sir Antony Fisher, is an educational charity, not a political organisation. It is independent of any political party or group and does not carry on activities intended to affect support for any political party or candidate in any election or referendum, or at any other time. It is financed by sales of publications, conference fees and voluntary donations.

In addition to its main series of publications the IEA also publishes a quarterly journal, *Economic Affairs*.

The IEA is aided in its work by a distinguished international Academic Advisory Council and an eminent panel of Honorary Fellows. Together with other academics, they review prospective IEA publications, their comments being passed on anonymously to authors. All IEA papers are therefore subject to the same rigorous independent refereeing process as used by leading academic journals.

IEA publications enjoy widespread classroom use and course adoptions in schools and universities. They are also sold throughout the world and often translated/reprinted.

Since 1974 the IEA has helped to create a world-wide network of 100 similar institutions in over 70 countries. They are all independent but share the IEA's mission.

Views expressed in the IEA's publications are those of the authors, not those of the Institute (which has no corporate view), its Managing Trustees, Academic Advisory Council members or senior staff.

Members of the Institute's Academic Advisory Council, Honorary Fellows, Trustees and Staff are listed on the following page.

The Institute gratefully acknowledges financial support for its publications programme and other work from a generous benefaction by the late Alec and Beryl Warren.

91

Other papers recently published by the IEA include:

WHO, What and Why?

Transnational Government, Legitimacy and the World Health Organization
Roger Scruton
Occasional Paper 113; ISBN 0 255 36487 3
£8.00

The World Turned Rightside Up

A New Trading Agenda for the Age of Globalisation
John C. Hulsman
Occasional Paper 114; ISBN 0 255 36495 4
£8.00

The Representation of Business in English Literature

Introduced and edited by Arthur Pollard
Readings 53; ISBN 0 255 36491 1
£12.00

Anti-Liberalism 2000

The Rise of New Millennium Collectivism
David Henderson
Occasional Paper 115; ISBN 0 255 36497 0
£7.50

Capitalism, Morality and Markets

Brian Griffiths, Robert A. Sirico, Norman Barry & Frank Field
Readings 54; ISBN 0 255 36496 2
£7.50

A Conversation with Harris and Seldon

Ralph Harris & Arthur Seldon
Occasional Paper 116; ISBN 0 255 36498 9
£7.50

Malaria and the DDT Story

Richard Tren & Roger Bate
Occasional Paper 117; ISBN 0 255 36499 7
£10.00

A Plea to Economists Who Favour Liberty: Assist the Everyman

Daniel B. Klein
Occasional Paper 118; ISBN 0 255 36501 2
£10.00

The Changing Fortunes of Economic Liberalism

Yesterday, Today and Tomorrow
David Henderson
Occasional Paper 105 (new edition); ISBN 0 255 36520 9
£12.50

The Global Education Industry

Lessons from Private Education in Developing Countries
James Tooley
Hobart Paper 141 (new edition); ISBN 0 255 36503 9
£12.50

Saving Our Streams

The Role of the Anglers' Conservation Association in
Protecting English and Welsh Rivers
Roger Bate
Research Monograph 53; ISBN 0 255 36494 6
£10.00

Better Off Out?

The Benefits or Costs of EU Membership
Brian Hindley & Martin Howe
Occasional Paper 99 (new edition); ISBN 0 255 36502 0
£10.00

Buckingham at 25

Freeing the Universities from State Control
Edited by James Tooley
Readings 55; ISBN 0 255 36512 8
£15.00

Lectures on Regulatory and Competition Policy

Irwin M. Stelzer

Occasional Paper 120; ISBN 0 255 36511 X

£12.50

Misguided Virtue

False Notions of Corporate Social Responsibility

David Henderson

Hobart Paper 142; ISBN 0 255 36510 1

£12.50

HIV and Aids in Schools

The Political Economy of Pressure Groups and Miseducation

Barrie Craven, Pauline Dixon, Gordon Stewart & James Tooley

Occasional Paper 121; ISBN 0 255 36522 5

£10.00

The Road to Serfdom

The Reader's Digest *condensed version*

Friedrich A. Hayek

Occasional Paper 122; ISBN 0 255 36530 6

£7.50

IEA Yearbook of Government Performance 2002/2003

Edited by Peter Warburton

Yearbook 1; ISBN 0 255 36532 2

£15.00

Britain's Relative Economic Performance, 1870–1999

Nicholas Crafts

Research Monograph 55; ISBN 0 255 36524 1

£10.00

Should We Have Faith in Central Banks?

Otmar Issing

Occasional Paper 125; ISBN 0 255 36528 4

£7.50

The Dilemma of Democracy

Arthur Seldon

Hobart Paper 136 (reissue); ISBN 0 255 36536 5

£10.00

Capital Controls: a 'Cure' Worse Than the Problem?

Forrest Capie

Research Monograph 56; ISBN 0 255 36506 3

£10.00

The Poverty of 'Development Economics'

Deepak Lal

Hobart Paper 144 (reissue); ISBN 0 255 36519 5

£15.00

Should Britain Join the Euro?

The Chancellor's Five Tests Examined

Patrick Minford

Occasional Paper 126; ISBN 0 255 36527 6

£7.50

Post-Communist Transition: Some Lessons

Leszek Balcerowicz

Occasional Paper 127; ISBN 0 255 36533 0

£7.50

A Tribute to Peter Bauer

John Blundell et al.

Occasional Paper 128; ISBN 0 255 36531 4

£10.00

Employment Tribunals

Their Growth and the Case for Radical Reform
J. R. Shackleton
Hobart Paper 145; ISBN 0 255 36515 2
£10.00

Fifty Economic Fallacies Exposed

Geoffrey E. Wood
Occasional Paper 129; ISBN 0 255 36518 7
£12.50

A Market in Airport Slots

Keith Boyfield (editor), David Starkie, Tom Bass & Barry Humphreys
Readings 56; ISBN 0 255 36505 5
£10.00

Money, Inflation and the Constitutional Position of the Central Bank

Milton Friedman & Charles A. E. Goodhart
Readings 57; ISBN 0 255 36538 1
£10.00

Corporate Governance: Accountability in the Marketplace
Elaine Sternberg
Second edition
Hobart Paper 147; ISBN 0 255 36542 X
£12.50

The Land Use Planning System
Evaluating Options for Reform
John Corkindale
Hobart Paper 148; ISBN 0 255 36550 0
£10.00

Economy and Virtue
Essays on the Theme of Markets and Morality
Edited by Dennis O'Keeffe
Readings 59; ISBN 0 255 36504 7
£12.50

Free Markets Under Siege
Cartels, Politics and Social Welfare
Richard A. Epstein
Occasional Paper 132; ISBN 0 255 36553 5
£10.00

Unshackling Accountants
D. R. Myddelton
Hobart Paper 149; ISBN 0 255 36559 4
£12.50

The Euro as Politics
Pedro Schwartz
Research Monograph 58; ISBN 0 255 36535 7
£12.50

Pricing Our Roads
Vision and Reality
Stephen Glaister & Daniel J. Graham
Research Monograph 59; ISBN 0 255 36562 4
£10.00

The Role of Business in the Modern World
Progress, Pressures and Prospects for the Market Economy
David Henderson
Hobart Paper 150; ISBN 0 255 36548 9
£12.50

Public Service Broadcasting Without the BBC?
Alan Peacock
Occasional Paper 133; ISBN 0 255 36565 9
£10.00

To order copies of currently available IEA papers, or to enquire about availability, please contact:

Lavis Marketing
IEA orders
FREEPOST LON21280
Oxford OX3 7BR

Tel: 01865 767575
Fax: 01865 750079
Email: orders@lavismarketing.co.uk

The IEA also offers a subscription service to its publications. For a single annual payment, currently £40.00 in the UK, you will receive every title the IEA publishes during the course of a year, invitations to events, and discounts on our extensive back catalogue. For more information, please contact:

Adam Myers
Subscriptions
The Institute of Economic Affairs
2 Lord North Street
London SW1P 3LB

Tel: 020 7799 8920
Fax: 020 7799 2137
Website: www.iea.org.uk